Kindred

Apuk Ayuel Mayen

Cover Art by Abul Oyay Deng Ajak.

To my mother
Josephine Paul Jurkin

TABLE OF CONTENTS

PART ONE
"Singing Songs Written in Accord to Fascinations"

PART TWO
"We All Discover In Loss Loving's Mesmeric Depths"

PART THREE
"Like A Glowing Moon, Enticing Yet Refraining"

WHISPERS OF THE HEART: AN INTRODUCTION

Poetry is a mysterious language that poets use when they do not want to speak loud. Sometimes poets deliberately avoid to say what they want to say, and Apuk Ayuel is no exception to this rule. In her poetry, you read a philosophical idealism beneath which lies ideology and mythology mixed with the expression of love and hope, which she projects into complex ideas that are difficult to discern. In most of her poems, one faces a variety of feelings. One of the prominent observations is clarity and sophistication of language as if she tells you while reading, "hear me clear."

The use of beautiful words sometimes with philosophical connotations suggests without a doubt that these words originated from an organized mind. Some of Apuk's ideas make her at par with masters of symbolism whose words are often humanely flavored with spiritually internalized thoughts. Some of the poems project Apuk as a patriotic trumpet, the voice of the unheard, the lone nationalist and a humanist salter. Elsewhere, you get the impression that the revolutionary tune of her poems agitates for continuity and the personification of continuity in her voice as "a luta continua."

In *Kindred*, you are faced with a wise orator, ready to give her soul for the prosperity of others, professing and inciting great ideas. Some of Apuk's poems reflect the hidden universality of spacelessness and time-lessness. She is everywhere, like an ascensionist angel, invisible, mobile and roaming with the wind. In these poems, Apuk lives in a harmonized yet conflicted mind, which is loving again hurting, and armed with a seductive voice. There is an invitation to wait for more. *Kindred* is indeed whispers of the heart.

John Gai Yoh
Juba, May 2018

PREFACE

Poetry, to me, is a companion, a confidant, an alter ego, a platform to bring to a catharsis that which is arrested, a freedom square to protest injustice, a place to animate the inanimate, a tombstone to eulogize the lost, and a canvass to glorify the ideal.

Herewithin are the reflections and revelations, celebrations and lamentations, fixations and commendations of a journey within. A journey in a quest to understand and be anchored in the essential "self," through evolution, regression, revolution, and stillness.

The human experience, though differentiated, is necessarily in pursuit of happiness, security, and belonging (LOVE). We all strive for these through finite wisdom and ways. I hope these verses inspire you, dear reader, to do your own reflections to grasp our spiritual essence and to strive to know love, its highs, and especially its lows.

Apuk Ayuel
Juba, May 2018

PART ONE

"Singing Songs Written in Accord to Fascinations"

ONE

Sunbake me in truth –
Skin commingled with flesh,
Thoughts ingrained in deeds.

ALTER OF ONENESS

Take a walk with me, barefoot,
With no destination in mind.
We'll fly upon the wings of a breeze,
And dive up into a cumulus cloud:

Be frozen, melted, and cleansed,
Over and over again.

Take a walk with me
Excited by the warmth of our clasp.
We'll plunge into the temple within,
And land upon the altar of oneness:

Be burned, melted, and fused,
Over and over again.

PSYCHIC ILLUSIONS

I built a glass house,
And surrounded it with rocks.
Something about our subconscious:
Better-hidden things are in the open, and
Better-guarded abodes are unfortified.

I built a stone house,
And decorated it with dynamite.
Something about our logic:
Most valuable things are concealed, and
Most luxurious abodes are garrisoned.

Come fire, come wind,
Everything that is death is also life, and
Be they accidents or fate,
Everything that is loss is also gain.

O' ineffable psychic illusions,
Equations in alarming disequilibrium.
Why not build a straw house,
And envelope it with the sun?

THE PLUNGE

Plunge
Soulfully,
Carelessly,
Even if you
Ostensibly loosen
The iron grip. O' champion
Spectator endowed with the allure
Of a kindred spirit. Experiment with this
Perfection divine. Regain the squandered potential
Of a seasoned stroke. Cast this bashful amateurism,
And that forged amorousness. Be motionless
Motion with the less motion of the
Inebriated. Let the primordial
Thirst-quencher overwhelm
Your addictions to
Submission, and
Envelope you
In this holy
Soulful
Plunge.

KEYS AND TURTLES

Lost in thoughts (of you),
Detached from being and matter,
And the matter of being.
Found in depths (of me),
Manifestations revealed, and
Revelations being manifested:

Springing in subtle explosions and
Quite eruptions,
Satiated by your touch, and
Our beings in communion.

Soaring in the bluest realms of skies, and
The blackest depths of oceans,
Where the second moon
Lies, thrives, and
Shines with a brilliance
Unknown, unfathomable.
More powerful than eyes can behold
Yet healing to the eye of my being,
Which shines,
Thrives, and
Lies in the ecstasy
Of deep comfort.

Witnessing revelations
Of dreams
In everything eye (I) behold -

Keys, spiritual guides,
Cats, turtles,
Bridges that lead into a temple
Of sacrifice, of healing,
Mirrors, and
An eye that zooms
Inward to read
Then outward to reflect.

BORROWED TIME

Search this darkness, oh my eyes –
Search ye for a reflection of your gaze.
Peer into this hollow mirror dimmed by brightness;
Fear not the faint possibilities of bliss.

But know ye that hope is –
A curse met with calmness;
Frozen impulses decreed to leap;
Living on borrowed time.

Rummage through reminiscences, oh my heart –
Rummage ye for a rhythm of your beats.
Pry into dense annals drowned in griminess;
March on in shallow progression to reprieve.

But know ye that hope is –
A curse met with calmness;
Frozen impulses decreed to leap;
Living on borrowed time.

ALAS

I dream of a pleasant breeze,
My heart at ease,
Palms open to receive.

I yearn for effortless collision,
Living in fusion,
Multiplying seeds of joy.

I fear to blink, lest I see flames flickering, and
Mute the rhythmic gratitude
Cascading in my breath.

I dream of a praiseworthy vision
On a noble mission
To restore me.

Alas.

STILL

I shatter into pieces,
No vessel to animate.
I am, still.

I am flying wind, saturated,
Colliding with everything.
I am, still.

Still, not moved nor moving,
Yet touching the infinite and expanding eternally.
Still, same now as will be yesterday and was tomorrow.

(For) Parameters matter only to those deluded by ill-sighted
Apparitions. These parameters mustn't para-shift
Your identity from essence to image.

What you see depends on many variables,
Like where the light hits the eye or when the subject
Becomes objectified enough to be measured.

More like, wrapped in chains, robbed of its oneness with
Everything; unable to be grasped by the deficient,
Extroverted perverted eyes.

Be still,
Invert your eyes, and
Grasp the expanse within.

I shatter to pieces,
Light as a feather.
I am, still.

I roam with the wind,
Carve the clouds, and yield.
I am, still.

LOST SCRIBE

Stranded in an earthly land of longing,
Fading in and out through a gateway of:

Slurred incantations, stupendously animating
The dormant in my being, and
Faint invocations fluently reclaiming
The mystical of my names.

Ushering to the fore:
Words lost in the labyrinth of memory,
Lives fused in the whirlwind of time, and
A face transfigured and transfixed evermore.

I am but a lost scribe,
Searching for an ethereal land of belonging.

SENSORY SENSE (CENTS)

Aren't the winds of change also retrogressive?
Who says time is linear, and
That there is really a timekeeper?

When the eternal dwell in the temporal,
Whose dictates are essential?
And aren't perceptions the only makers of reality?

A frog indwelling in an eagle's frame can only soar if it
Perceives itself as an eagle. And an eagle indwelling in
A frog's frame is eternally imprisoned by the limits of its host.

Woe is she who is realized
But entrapped in a lesser vehicle,
When she succumbs to the limits of time and space.

THE SUITE CASE

My beloved seeks comfort from
A time-capsule encasing:

Visions of morrows,
And relics of yester sorrows;
Whispers of comfort,
And immortal words
Of immortal souls
Lost to the present;

Tears unshed,
And goodbyes unsaid;
Long gone love returning,
And repressed hurt forgiving;
And the caged flying, soaring,
In yester dreams
Of promising morrows.

A suitcase,a gift that keeps on giving
In silent, lonesome reflections.

ROAD TO DESTINY

We must mature,
Discover where we are going.
We must shed away this scar,
Be renewed us, you and me; we are
Sowing towards a future
Of generations with true culture.

Don't let pride slow and cripple you.
Admit your faults, and move away
From your bags of guilt and shame,
The yoke on your mind and frame.

Awakening the powerful soul,
Your force and the control
That has been suppressed to fray,
Surfacing in this very day
Of some-thing and some-body.
Assuring you that you'll birth
Your potential and claim your inheritance,
Relinquishing your fears and reluctance.

So when you emerge from the shell,
Freed from this metamorphosis hell,
With hardly any wrinkle or blemish.
Rejoice you are about to astonish!

Alas, we are realizing our destiny, and
Becoming what we were meant to be.

ONENESS

I heard your voice
In the whispers of the wind,
Calling me to the ends of the earth
Where the horizon meets the ground,
Where all material lose form, and
Dissipate into thin air.

There, where we'll be submerged in
The great light of wholeness.
There, where we'll cease anticipation and
Enjoy every bit of being.

Oneness isn't it what we crave?
Isn't it what we toil for?
Oneness with the beginning.

I felt your touch
In the movement of sun rays dancing across my face,
Comforting me through yet another dreadful hour.
Within each second I ached for the beginning of eternity.
Within each minute I trod millions of steps
Towards the ultimate.

There, where we'll be submerged in
The great light of wholeness.
There where we'll cease anticipation and
Enjoy every bit of being.

Oneness isn't it what we crave?
Isn't it what we toil for?
Oneness with the end.

I saw your face
In the center of a blooming flower,
Revealing to me beauty unrivaled,
Inspiring me to expose the seed implanted within,
Allowing it to germinate, and
Reflect the lulu, I am in you.

There where we'll be submerged in
The great light of wholeness.
There where we'll cease anticipation and
Enjoy every bit of being.

Oneness is what we crave;
It is what we toil for.
Oneness with the beginning and the end.

MEDITATION I

The spirit is strong,
Anchored,
Stirred only by
True word, and
True motion.

Heeding to that
In all things;
Knowing that true sight
Has no eyes, and true hearing
Has no ears.

The spirit is before,
Above, and
After the letter.

Essence is not
Merely the reflection.
It's before, above,
Beneath and beyond
This fleshy manifestation:
The temple
The tool
The extension
The enclosure
The separator
The identifier
The statehood
The Dominion

The spirit is strong,
Anchored,
Stirred only by
True word, and
True motion.

MEDITATION II

Invert your sight:
Find seeds for deeds
In the invisible orchards
Of the All.

Reverse your tongue:
Shed words of swords
In the bottomless sea
Of the Naught.

Sublimate your energy:
Change regression's emissaries
Into the providential conspirators
Of ascension.

Secure your peace:
Re-legion with your SELF
In the undifferentiated state
Of ATEM/AMEN.

WHERE AM I TO HIDE?

In the darkness of my alleys,
They crown me mistress of light.
In the thickness of my fog,
They coin me most transparent.

Where am I to hide?

DIVINITY

Priesthood divine,
Supreme nature,
Reminiscent of the primordial being,
God-given blessing to earth, sky, and sea.

Water untainted,
Coded in its first composition,
Elevates to the first position,
Heals every lesion, and
Neutralizes every poison.

Wo(man) receive your rain:
Let every drop sate your every grain, and
Activate every vessel of creation within
Your nature supreme,
Divine priesthood.

I AM HERE FOR YOU

Blessed assuredness, take root.
Shed this recklessness –

"Slow and steady
Only when ready,
I AM here for you."

Singing songs
Written in accord
To fascinations,
Risen a pitch or two
Above hallucinations.

"Tempered craze,
Mired grace,
I AM here for you."

Speaking words
Uttered in tones
Of nerving nuance,
Fashioned in call and response,
In the flood tide of a séance.

"Timid restitution,
Detached absolution,
I AM here for you."

BE THE FLAME

Hey you, timid soul,
Come to the fold!
Yes, you hugging the sidelines;
The center is home.

Fear, not your molten core. Cloak your shell
With your insides; be the flame!
Listen not to these wise fools,
Spewing fabrications as truths.

Follow not these middlemen of doom, pressed
To down-press those whose hearts are weightless.
It is ordained since the end that you be
An oracle of hope with the sharp edge of a pruning knife.

There is no absolution for the fearful betrayer of destiny;
The willfully mute, the willfully blind.
No absolution for bystanders, for all are actors,
Be they detractors, contractors, or reactors.

Look in the mirror,
See your raging soul looking back.
Dim not your light,
The fire breath within you.

PART TWO
"WE ALL DISCOVER IN LOSS LOVING'S MESMERIC DEPTHS"

YOUR NAME

Beloved, your name is
An incessant whisper
Beckoning me to secret alleys
Of forgotten dreams.

UNTITLED #9

Serenity of deep waters,
Warmth of a womb's embrace –
O' how I crave to entwine
The glimmer of your eyes.

Inspiration of soaring heights,
Vivacity of surging waves –
O' how I yearn to rival
The cadence of your laugh.

I SIGH (LOVE'S CIRCLE)
For True Love

I want you
I need you
I feel you
I crave you
I like you
I love you
I see you
I sigh.

I want you king in my life
I need you strength by my side
I feel you hurting inside
I crave you thriving beside (me)
I like you indeed
I love you in degrees
I see you in my soul
I sigh.

You want a sister
You need support
You feel disappointed
You crave growth
You like everything I am
You love I in the 3rd degree
You see below the surface
You sigh.

I be your Auset eternally
I give you rebirth

I revive your belief
I nourish your potential
I like everything you are
I love you in the 7th degree
I see beyond the limits
I sigh.

You be my Ausar naturally
You give I seed
You revive my dreams
You nourish my trees
You like everything I am
You love I in the 7th degree
You see I in your soul
You sigh.

You want I
You need I
You feel I
You crave I
You like I
You Love I
You see I
You sigh.

HOLLOW CONVERSATIONS

The release of pint up tension
The instance hello parts your lips,
And enters my eardrums.
That timely word filling a moment of void,
Extenuated by my longing to melt in your eyes,
Concealed in that sigh, and arrested the second I speak.

Not saying what the heart screams
Amplified a thousand times by its pounding beats.
Just empty words traveling on shallow air,
Falling on a receptor programmed to respond
Only to that which is arrested by timidity,
Echoed by the soul, but never uttered by
Two silent lovers, engaged in hollow conversations.

THE FORBIDDEN

Eyes shining with beauty,
Right-leaning in duty;
Naught is sweeter
Than the forbidden.

Reminisces of the last sighting
Captured in cyclical time, and
Daydreams of future thieving
Rehearsed in theatrical prime.

Voice clinging to longing,
Left-leaning in belonging;
Naught is sweeter
Than the forbidden.

LOVE IS ETERNAL

This now wildly exploding chest ache
Is the then deep heart hurt hid
Beyond prying doubtful eyes.

This now sullied heart clinging love
Is the then pure being love leaping
Towards expectant open arms.

All time happens at the same time.
Love is eternal.

JUXTAPOSITIONS

Juxtapose life to its end,
Joy to grief, and
Pain to relief.
What would you get?
Hails of a storm,
Or mists of dew?

Juxtapose presence to absence,
Giving to receiving, and
Loving to hurting.
What would you miss?
Silent Smiles
Or echoing goodbyes?

Juxtapose me to you,
Ego to heart, and
Fence to guard.
What would you find?
Haughtiness of love,
Or prejudice of pride?

INSOMNIAC FEAT

In the stillness of this sleepless night,
I murdered hopeless hope
With the sharpness of sensibilities,
Reticent and crude.

Dear I, dare I take in the sight of I,
Bloodstained, victim and vicious slayer?

Enfold this crime, shall I,
In a memory entrenched yet lost,
Encoded in dispassionate recalls,
Apt and obscure.

SHUN ME NOT

Shun me not, beloved.
Push me not to the sharp edges of estrangement.

For tomorrow, overcome by so fierce a desperation,
Delve you will into piles of garments sweat-scented
In the passion of forgotten days, in search for me.

DREAMS OF POSSESSION

Loving is
Cherished pain
Even for
The feeble-hearted.

We are encoded to crave
Companionship, though
We oft perfect (oppressive)
Co-dependency.
The passion
Quickening
Our quivering,
Has no qualms
About either the
Dreams of possession,
Or the gnawing
Poisoning
Loving's
Purest
Manifestations.

The pure-hearted,
On this fabled trail,
Seeing the wounds of some
Mistrials – witless –
Retreat inwardly to memories
Of the womb's embrace.

Disappointments
Heralding
Heartbreaks,
Testify of
Fervency.

Alienated lovers
Restored
In parallel
Worlds.
Eager suitors
Sustained
By the promise of
A gleaming smile.
Wandering souls
Obsessing with
Perfecting
Imitations.
We all discover
In loss
Loving's
Mesmeric depths.

Loving is
Cherished torment
Even for
The strong-headed.

WHEN GUARDIANS BETRAY TRUST

Here is a whip;
Lie down for a hundred lashes on your body,
A thousand more on your soul, and
How you just lost the memory of
The sweetest kiss.

Here is a hand;
Bear its force on your face two times,
An earthquake on your mind, and
Oh, there goes the best friend
You met today.
Lost in the abyss of memory
Repressed, caged.

Here is a foot,
Let it kick you five times against this wall of steel,
Twice more against that wall of thorns, and
There goes the innocence of childhood
Locked forever in this bloody room
Where guardians murder the very soul of those
They're entrusted to protect.

There goes sweet trust, and
Here come walls and walls and walls
That lockout:
The creeping sense of bewilderment seeking to surface,
The sweet innocent smiles of a sanguine heart, and
The leaping memory of endless laughter and joy
Of a frozen kerkede (hibiscus) summer afternoon.

There goes that kiss, sweet,
But wasted on these numb lips.
Here comes gloom,
Sadness, cages, thorns, and blood.
Flooding memories of the abyss.
And now you are your guardian
Murdering your very own soul.

LOVE KNOWS

Love is, an unquenchable thirst
Longing to be swallowed by a well,
An insatiable hunger
Waiting to be consumed by a savored.

Love is endlessly longing to know, and
Helplessly waiting to grasp, itself.

Love knows,
We never really touch;
Our rhyme and rhythm
Is pursue and elude.

PREMONITION

Fire blazing,
Breathless,
Shut within:
Feeding the hunger, and
Quenching the thirst.

Famished
You'd return, and
In ashes
We'd be fused.

THE SULTRY SWAY

He stands there,
Still, reverent,
As if in holy presence.
He envelops her
Wholly in his world , and
For a brief moment
He dares not blink.
He says a prayer,
While She strings words
Into a story, two and three:

"Hallowed is the day
Our paths danced the sultry sway,
Daring us not to be hooked
On the nectar of this fruit
Fertilized in fields of radiating spirits,
Drenched in thanksgiving and
Anchored in awe of love,
Unspoken, untouched.

"Hallowed is She that
Speaks in keeping with this pulse.
Hollowed is She that
Pierces these dreams with sounds
Sweeter than nocturnal love
Songs of mockingbirds.
Hallowed is She.
Hallowed is this day."

Her chattering
Breaks the air, and
Her unrestrained laughter
Gives the wind its waves.
Beneath her steady gaze
Lie secrets
She dares not reveal.
She says a prayer,
While He strings thoughts
Into a vision, two and three:

"Hallowed is the day
Our paths danced the sultry sway,
Daring us not to be hooked
On the nectar of this fruit
Fertilized in fields
Of radiating spirits,
Drenched in thanksgiving and
Anchored in awe of love,
Unspoken, untouched.

"Hallowed is He that
Speaks in keeping with this pulse.
Hollowed is He that
Pierces these dreams with sounds
Sweeter than nocturnal love
Songs of mockingbirds.
Hallowed is He.
Hallowed is this day."

He is Rhapsody
Mindful of future yearnings,
She is harmony
Veiling vibrations of churning:
Dancing the sultry sway.

SHE

She
Lost the thing that animates and moves her
To fully be free in bondage and bonded in freedom.

She
Is cut to pieces trying to shadow the thousand shreds
Of her beloved broken heart.

She bleeds to re-stain him to life.

DARK MATTER

I met this sun, light years away from its beginning,
A ball of self-consuming flame
In a perpetual manifestation of brilliance.

Awestruck, can't begin to describe
My state of being. And then, Yo,
It tried to lick me with its fiery tongue!

But little did it know that
I am a phantom of its future obsession, encoded in
Its perpetual intercession for the beloved.

The blind that I see is looking for...me?
The blind that don't see is looking for...me!

A masquerade tumbling in search of a concussion to jolt
Its being back to blindness, shunning the parade of enticing rust, and
Consuming its fiery tongue to whisper smoke into my dreams:

...Cats, turtles, and bridges,
...Cats, turtles, and bridges,
...Cats, turtles, and bridges

...And that key imprinted on the tips its rays seek from me
Through soils: a husband, a prophet, and a priest. The one to
Bring nurturing, the one to sow awakening, the one to speak blessing.

But, the blind that I see is looking for...me.
The blind that don't see is looking for...me?

Had to leave him nestled in his temple, awakening his third chakra.
I am the beginning and the end: the purity he seeks, the
Peace he needs, the depth he craves, and the death he braves.

Lost into myself till such a day a collision manifests conditions for
An amnesiac awakening, a return to the essential
I recede to envelope that sun.

For the blind that I see is looking for...me.
The blind that don't see is looking for...me.

CLOUDS

The dark clouds have lifted.
No longer will I look to the
Past with gloom. Nor will I
Project upon yesterday dreams
Of a tomorrow with you.

The pregnant clouds have poured and
Released with its birthing pains,
A heart renewed and a mind reviewed.
Solid in understandings and
Eager for undertakings:

Of simple joys of
Crashing into him
As seamless as a stream
Into a river;
Of warmth of
Leaping Hearts; and of
A meeting of minds
Dancing in reverie.

Words stumbling
Eager to be spoken,
Eyes meeting in
Sweet reluctance,
A flame kindled.

Gone are the days of living
In the shadows of regret.

Gone are the days where
Dreams of tomorrows
Oppressed my heart with grief.
I am free of a prison manned by the fear
Of imagining afresh;
Free of a mind haunted by memories
Of joys and laughter of days gone.

No longer will I move in a tunnel of doom,
Where ghost rioters of the past choke me
In the present.
I will scoop this cloud and mold that cloud, and
When it rains, I will thrust my tears
Into heaven.
I will dream anew,
Imagine afresh, and
Delve into
Simple Joys.

PART THREE

"LIKE A GLOWING MOON, ENTICING YET RE-FRAINING"

YOUR LAUGH

Steady roars of a lion, satiated.
Soulful incantations of spirits, materializing.
Harmonic melodies ever evoking
Hypnotic notes in my depths.

NILE SCENE

Oh, the healing sounds of water gushing and rushing into the Nile:
Bubbles, ripples and endless waves cascading melodiously:
Yielding, dissipating, reforming, sinking and resurfacing eternally.

And oh, the edifying sight of mangoes, over-ripened, thunderously
Kissing the ground, ants dutifully marching in a metrical pace, and
Flowers fiercely budding through the shackles of concrete.

SON OF THE LAND

Velvet black skin,
Divine stature;
Beloved of the sun
Through whom creation gifts flow.

Resounding voice
Emanating from the depth of a soul
Grounded in roots,
Connected to the core.

Wicked innocence
Enticing essences to forsake
The vanity of thoughtful cowardice, and
That of thoughtless bravado.

Pure zealousness
For the trunk, branches,
Leaves, and fruits
Of our great family tree.

Son of the land:

The velvet in your black skin
Is the source of my light.
The resonance of your voice
Is the drum for my dance.

The wickedness of your innocence
Is the acme in my laugh.
The purity of your zeal
Is the crown on my head.

KINDRED

Kindred in spirit and mind,
I cherish you.

Reward of heavens
At the thought of you –
Akin to an oracle's affirmation
Unto a crazed muse, and
A Muse's inspiration
Unto an inhibited scribe –
I leap in flow
Like a river into an ocean,
Blessedly rejoicing
Our multiplicities of
Connected incarnations,
Pleasantly resounding,
In awe,
In grace.

Kindred in spirit and mind
I cherish you.

DAYDREAMS

You on my mind, I twirl
Like a child invigorated
By the rush of a cool breeze, and
Soar like a bird's zealousness
About the heights of its first flight.

You on my mind,
An aphrodisiac arousing
The zest for a blissful kiss of life.
You lure me, like a child to
A playground, and like a dove to
A trusted feeder's hand.

You on my mind, I am drawn
As to a magnet eternally
Challenging life to dare separate us, and
Dive like loneliness'
Abandonment towards the
Memories of the womb's embrace.

You on my mind,
A seductive thought of joys
Multiplied by the vision your smile.
You entice me, like a child to
A playground, and like a dove to
A gentle feeder's hand.

COLORLESS

For Aduei Riak

Are you really colorless, and
I the multiplicities of color?
Then how do you rivet me
In a rapture of enchantments?

Frighten not your eagerness
To rest in my tukul**; twist
Your tongue in imitation of mine,
As mimicry leads to mastery.
You will learn to speak
And live like I do, so long as love binds.

Do not mind my kin, they
Forget that a woman has no tribe.
She makes her home with her man, and
If blessed, she is crowned
In burial with his ancestors.

They say you are colorless, and
Worse: you do not know our ways.
Crown me, dear colorless, as you wish.
Honor my people with tethering cattle
In their byres. May their joy overflow!

Observe our ways
That you may soften their hearts,
So they may greet you with endearment and

---

* A hut in Sudanese colloquial Arabic, origin Turkish.

Not in the detached deference
Accorded strangers.

Do not mind my beloved people;
They fear for me as a woman.
I may be mistreated in your land,
Faraway, across rivers they cannot even name.

Worse, they fear you may desert me
With half-colored children –
Leaving my kin without honor
And me full of shame.

Never mind, I tell my people –
The colorless rivets me
In a rapture of enchantments;
I am filled with colorful visions
Of a live enriched and horizons stretched.

Love, after all, is colorless and
Multiplicities of color at the same time.

I will frighten not my eagerness
To rest in your home. I will twist
My tongue in imitation of yours,
As mimicry leads to mastery.
I will learn to speak
And live like you do, so long as love binds.

YOUR VOICE

Smokey whispers of ages ago,
Riding waves of northern winds
Oscillating in the ecstasy of intercourses
With magnificent trees of ancients.

Soft echoes of times to come,
Entwined with beats of tribal drums
Resounding in the intensity of trance-dances
With ever-present spirits of ancients.

Your voice,
Sways me.

ENIGMA

Shy, soft, and reluctant.
In subtlety, he bore his heart, timidly.
He stole glances here and there,
Looked away, when he wanted to stare.

He painted pictures in his mind
Upon the glimpses of his eyes, and
From the twinkle that he can't hide,
I can tell he is etching blue skies
For a wondrous land.

Intrigued by his silence, and
Puzzled by his choice to exist unnoticed,
I questioned how he glides through life unvoiced;
From the perceptions of my mind,
I labeled him: Enigma.

FORGIVE ME FATHER

Forgive me, father, for I have sinned,
All my virtues were gone with the wind.
The instant I laid my eyes on him,
I knew I was his missing limb.

Bless me father, he smiled,
I mustn't show him that I'm beguiled.
He looked my way, and I've melted.
Or is it that my dress is tightly belted?

Oh my lord, don't cause me to be stricken,
Our timely meeting I want to quicken.
If he be from thee, he'll stare.
Otherwise, for another look, he won't care.
I pray o' father; he'd go no further,
For surely my heartbeat will cease, and
From the grip of gloom, I won't find release.

Grant me courage O' Lord,
His missing limb must be restored.
Father, I know according to your will,
My heart's desire you will fulfill.

For now, glue me together, I'm trembling,
Because all my visions he is resembling.
Alas, he be a phantom of my imagination,
Arising from my need, a mere aberration.

Oh, how I ache for his immediate proximity,
Seems he and I, are operating in unanimity.
When my thirst for him becomes unbearable,
He quickly soaks me with affection, oh he's terrible.

The second my hope is spent,
He appears, just like a heaven's sent.
Forgive me, father, for I have sinned,
All my actions I wish to rescind.

I AM THE ONE THEY LOVE TO HATE

I am the one
They love to hate.
They sing my praises,
Seek my graces,
But they are doomed to vacillate
From that which they try to imitate.
Better spend the time to originate;
No other way to levitate
To where I be.
Cause I see
What I am, as perfect imperfection
Living in holistic affection,
Never seeking attention,
Cause I be
Where I see.
You dig?

Then dig deep within;
Find the will to grin
Even with a crooked chin.
You are a beauty,
Being me is a duty.
I embody a mere possibility,
A testament to life's divisibility, and
Seemingly frail invincibility.
It's agility
Mistaken for debility.
I am nobility

Respect my civility,
But regard not my tranquility
A weakness,

For when my wrath quickness,
There won't be revisions
To the trajectory of my munitions.
Woe they who oppose
The upright and suppose
Victory,
No amount of trickery
Or auxiliary
Would lessen their misery.
You dig?

Better see
Where I be,
An inspiration,
Not for blind imitation;
For, for each her limitation.
Ye art thy only rival,
Yet ye elect to self-stifle,
In singing my praises, and
Seeking my graces.
Damn, I am the one
They love to hate!

MUNDARI GIRL

Na Ku'da *–
Where did you learn such grace?
How do you walk so unhurriedly,
As if the wind is your invisible usher?
And these ŋaalia† adorning
The brilliance of your black opal skin,
Why are they more enchanting
Than diamonds can ever dream be?

Na Muni –
Where did you find such poise?
How do you stand so majestically,
As if sun rays are your adoration songs?
And that tyuli† highlighting
The splendor of your tightly curled crown,
Why is it more attractive
Than hair weaves can ever aim be?

Na Tali –
Where does the well of beauty lie?
How do you glow so effortlessly
As if the fountain of youth is your private spring?

---

*Na means 'that of' (feminine), or 'daughter of' in the Bari Language. K'uda/Muni/Tali, are names of Mundari villages in South Sudan.

†A word meaning "beads" in the Bari Language of South Sudan

‡A word for a particular hairstyle found in many places in Africa and worn by many tribes in South Sudan, whereby the head is shaved save for a circular crown.

And these white kala* multiplying
The intrigue of your genial smile,
Why are they more entrapping
Than sophisticated words can ever dare be?

---

*A word meaning "teeth" in the Bari Language of South Sudan

YOUR NECK

Says the Nilotic to his eternal darling –
Your eyes,
Enchanting jewels
Dazzling with the memories and
Epiphanies of lifetimes of entwining,
Enthralls me.

Your lips,
Scrumptious fruits
Ripe with the anticipations and
Deprivations of infinities of longing,
Rivets me.

But your neck!
Your neck,
Most
Cherished
Immaculate being!

Your neck,
Enchanting corridors
Accentuated with the ascents and
Descents of perpetuities of surrender,
Beckons me.

THAT'S JUST ME

Mahogany sun-kissed skin,
Majestically framed inch by inch;
Wild locks as stubborn as can be,
Yeah, that's me!
Gleaming eyes penetrating your being,
Sending waves of electricity through
Your mainstream.
Shocked and regenerated is what you'd be –

For I am exuding femininity in every strut, and
I am sensed with eyes wide shut.
The complexity is the fatal attraction, and
Your perplexity is the natural reaction.
Confidence is the seal, and it's in
The way that I deal, in the little that I reveal, and
In the little that I conceal.
That's just me!

I'm not a riddle,
So you need not fiddle
This mystic, holistic, and artistic
Manifestation of me.
I'm simplistic, never sadistic.
So be realistic and appreciate
Because you can't depreciate,
What's just me!

TOGETHER

She guards the den like a lioness;
He seeks her like the faint gasps for air.

She spoon-feeds him her soul;
He bathes in her luminescence.

Admittedly captivated,
Amateurishly indulgent,

Together.

NHOAKÁ JI ÉLONG

If I could chirp like a bird,
I would sing you the sweetest of songs.
A song peppered with gladness,
Salted with joyous tears, and
Simmered in my endless affection for thee.
But with the frailty of my voice,
I would only be able to say
In the sweetest of tongues:
Nhoaká ji élong*.

---

* A phrase meaning, "I love you dearly" in the Nuer Language of South Sudan.

VISIONS AND DREAMS

Night visions and daydreams
Will they ever come to pass?
Living blissfully in my thoughts,
Reality I do surpass.

Be it a minute, an hour or eternity,
With no question, I'll relinquish now in its entirety;
For a chance to have a picnic on the moon, and
To kiss you till you swoon.

To be lost in a country paradise
In a state of innocence with no guise.
To be one with all that is natural
Where what's primitive is casual.

No rules, no laws, no regulation,
Plenty for everyone's fancy, beyond imagination.
Love will be the sole guiding principle, and
Nature the only municipal.

THE ONE

You are the one
Who lures me
To fall in gratitude,
Into a bottomless pit,
Into a perpetual surrender.

The one who stirs me
To whirl in quietude,
Into an effortless bliss,
Into an eternal ember.

You are the one,
Who secures me
To plunge in latitude,
Into a limitless sea,
Into a fertile slumber.

The one who roots me
To seed in fortitude,
Into a fearless dream,
Into a boundless splendor.

WOMAN

Woman, thou art
Like a gentle dew,
Permeating yet enveloping;
Like a glowing moon,
Enticing yet refraining.

Thou art like a flowing river,
Yielding yet elusive.

Thou art
Help and challenge,
Sustenance and hunger.
Hearts leap into your palms, and
Desires twinkle in your eyes.

Thou art providence and measure;
Life blossoms in your enfold.

www.ingramcontent.com/pod-product-compliance
Lightning Source LLC
Chambersburg PA
CBHW031539040426
42445CB00010B/609